George Edward Lodge

An Artist's Perspective on Falconry

George Edward Lodge Trust
www.georgeedwardlodgetrust.co.uk

George Edward Lodge

An Artist's Perspective on Falconry

Edited by George Edward Lodge Trust

First published 2009 by
George Edward Lodge Trust

British Library Cataloguing Publication data
A catalogue record for this book is available from the British Library

ISBN: 978-0-9562946-0-9

First Edition

Printed in Great Britain by J F Print Ltd. Sparkford, Yeovil.

Front cover 'Hooded peregrine falcon', George Edward Lodge Trust logo. Painted in 1891 by G.E. Lodge.

Acknowledgments

The George Edward Lodge Trust is extremely grateful to the following for their kind help, and support:

Karen Bird

Wildlife photographer (Stewart Canham)

Surrey Heath Museum, Camberley (Sharon Cross)

Archive of Falconry, USA (Peter Devers)

Martyn Hopwood

Charles Mann

Douglas Mann

Michael Mann

The late Harry Savory

John Southern

R.F. Stratton, OBE

Tryon Gallery, London (Oliver Swann)

Red Kite Design (Gordon Templeton)

Dick Treleaven, MBE

G.E.L. Trust Sponsor (June Woodford)

G.E.L. Trust Sponsor (Michael Woodford)

Bird Control Unit Staff, RNAS Yeovilton

The British Falconers' Club

Special thanks to Oliver Swann, Michael and June Woodford, whose encouragement and generosity have been considerable, with the establishment of the newly formed George Edward Lodge Trust.

We also would like to thank the advertisers who appear in the book without whom this publication would not have been possible.

The Trust would like to thank falconers, admirers past and present for any material in this publication that has not been acknowledged. The Trustees hope you accept their sincere apologies.

Dedication

TO THE MEMORY OF THE LATE
THOMAS J. MANN
OF HYDE HALL, SAWBRIDGEWORTH, HERTFORDSHIRE

*'WITH WHOM GEORGE EDWARD LODGE
FOUND FALCONRY AND FRIENDSHIP...'*

Information about the George Edward Lodge Trust

www.georgeedwardlodgetrust.co.uk
email: info@georgeedwardlodgetrust.co.uk

Aims of the Charity:

To advance education of the public in the artwork, life and skills of
George Edward Lodge.

Activities:

The website is devoted to portraying all aspects of the life of G.E. Lodge
and will include:

- Biographical information
- Reproductions of his artwork
- Representations of his diaries and memorabilia belonging to him

The Trust will build up a directory of artwork and artefacts relating to G.E. Lodge,
endeavouring to determine what is available, where it is located and whether it is
possible to be viewed.

The Trust will make available artwork and artefacts for those wishing to gain a
greater understanding of G.E. Lodge, his artwork and techniques.

The Trust will build up an historical picture of Falconry in the 19th and early 20th
centuries based particularly upon the artwork, records and diaries of G.E. Lodge,
but expanding to incorporate other sources as they become available.

Trustees:

Contact us:

The Trust welcomes support from anyone interested in the
life and works of George Edward Lodge.

Please contact: Brian Bird, George Edward Lodge Trust,
P.O. Box 1583, Bourton, Gillingham SP8 5WX

Tel: 01747 840923

The Trust needs your support to succeed

George Edward Lodge
1860-1954

From George Lodge's *Memoirs of an Artist Naturalist*

The world which studies birds...

The world which studies birds has sought out George E. Lodge to good purpose. Those who can appreciate this wonderful combination of painstaking study and artistic genius have used his paintings in many publications that are known to have the stamp of authority, for those drawings have a two-fold value, they are a delight to the casual beholder and at the same time satisfy the critical eye of the expert ornithologist. Birds and their surroundings are faithfully reproduced.

Preface

George Edward Lodge – The Collector's View

Painting was by no means the only obsession of this truly remarkable genius but it is certainly the sphere in which he is most widely acclaimed today. In 1959, five years after his death, the Hon Aylmer Tryon founded his eponymous Gallery and for some 50 years the Gallery has exhibited the very best of the world's sporting and naturalist painters. Lodge, together with Archibald Thorburn and Joseph Wolf, has always maintained unrivalled status as one of the precursors of today's generation of painters.

Painting in this genre requires not only artistic ability but also acute observation and in-depth knowledge of all aspects of the subjects depicted. Such a challenge was only too welcome by such a devotee as GEL. His paintings are as glorious as they are interesting, and as a Gallery we have been involved in collecting and exhibiting Lodge's work over the past half century. This is a tradition which we are very pleased to continue.

For as long as we share Nature's realm without destroying it, the world of GEL will remain a fascinating heritage known through his diaries and paintings, and we are immensely proud to be part of this continuing awareness.

Oliver Swann
G.E.L. *Trust Trustee and Proprietor of Tryon Gallery*

Oliver Swann.

Foreword

Dick Treleaven, M.B.E. *George Lodge's last pupil*

George Edward Lodge 1860-1954; A Memoir

In the late 1940's, when wandering down Piccadilly, my eye was taken by some paintings of falcons in Rowland Ward's window. The pictures portrayed cold, sharp-eyed, gyr falcons perched atop of lichen covered boulders, staring out into Arctic wastes. A welcome change from the plethora of ducks endlessly flighting against purple sunsets, which frequently adorn the walls of suburbia. I decided there and then, that this was the way I wanted to paint. I asked the Hon. Aylmer Tryon, a director of the gallery, if it would be possible to meet the artist. He gave me George Lodge's address and suggested that I wrote to him.

On my return to Cornwall I did so, and was delighted to receive a reply by return of post saying, 'I am 88 and don't wander far. Come anytime.'

It was only then that I learnt that Lodge was not only the foremost painter of birds of prey in Europe, but a contemporary of Archibald Thorburn and Bruno Liljefors (all born in 1860). The die was cast, and on a wintry afternoon in November I nervously made my way up the drive of Hawkhouse, Camberley. Brenda, his niece, who acted as his housekeeper, opened the door. She wore a long black dress with a white embroidery anglais collar as would befit an elderly Victorian maiden lady. She made me welcome, offering me a cup of coffee, and warned me that the previous day someone had told her uncle that he looked like Bernard Shaw and he was not amused.

Aladdin's Cave

I was led into his vast, high-roofed studio the size of a small gymnasium, which was full of mounted specimens of falcons and game birds in glass cases, huge oil paintings hanging from the ceiling and large wooden cabinets containing his collections of bird skins. At the far end, huddled in front of a gas fire sat the great man: a patch over one eye, looking like a pirate. Clad in his magnificent old green hawking jacket with the brass buttons, he was contentedly smoking his pipe. He rose from his chair and shook me warmly by the hand. I was like a small boy who had accidentally stumbled into Aladdin's cave. I tried to take it all in but there was just too much of everything.

I had brought with me a selection of my most recent watercolour paintings. He went through them one by one, gently pointing out the errors of my ways and explaining that I must try and improve my knowledge of the way feathers were grouped. Going to a cabinet he took out the skin of a drake teal and showed me how each scapular overlapped the one next to it when he closed its wing. The next three hours passed in a flash. He told me he could not teach anyone to paint, as 'he dashed about too much', but I was welcome to watch him at work.

It was during this first meeting that I learnt that as a young man he had been much influenced by the work of the legendary Joseph Wolf. With a twinkle in his eye he told me,

'I liked visiting his studio as he always gave me a glass of whisky.' Questioning him further he told me that Wolf used to complain that John Gould, the unscrupulous producer of lavish and exotic nineteenth century bird books, frequently visited him and stole his sketches from which his wife would make engravings, leaving a cigar on the table as a token payment. Listening to these magical tales from the past was, for me, a kind of apostolic succession.

When it was time for me to catch my train back to London, he walked slowly down the drive with me. His final words as he bade me good night were, 'We painters should be allowed to live to be at least a thousand years, then perhaps we could get an inkling of our trade.' My ego rose a hundred per cent as I walked back to the railway station in the dark.

Inner Sanctum

I was to become a frequent visitor to Hawkhouse until his death at the age of ninety-three in 1954. If the light was too poor for him to paint we would retire to his inner sanctum, his study, which was lined with shelf upon shelf of finely bound books. On one there was a row of thick volumes all entitled *Grouse in Sickness and in Health.* When Dr Edward Wilson perished in Antarctica he had been studying grouse disease. His scientific papers were then re-edited by W.R. Ogilvie-Grant, part of which was published in the 1912 *British Game Birds & Wildfowl (The Gun at Home and Abroad Vol 1).* George Lodge painted all the plates, which are some of the finest examples of his work as a bird illustrator.

I was curious to know about his relationship with the taciturn Archibald Thorburn. He acknowledged that Thorburn was an extremely skilful watercolourist and always received a far higher price for his illustrations than he did; then added a trifle mischievously, 'But I *knew* much more than he did.' He admired the work of Bruno Liljefors, the Swedish painter, who was influenced by the French Impressionists and considered him to be the greatest of all the wildlife painters; an opinion that is shared by many today. Of modern artists he was a little scathing, saying some of them seem to use cement instead of paint, and their paintings were all too frequently petrified with accuracy and completely lifeless.

Feathers & Bones

One of the reasons why Lodge has always been so revered by falconers is because he often painted individual birds, birds that were readily recognised by their owners. Skins he said were only useful to show the effects of light not to copy from.

He was emphatic that birds must be depicted with shadow under them and that the shadow must contain reflected light in order for it to become convincing. One has only to look at Lodge's bird to sense that it is made of feathers and there were bones beneath its skin. They were alive and not stuffed, or cast in concrete. Every blade of grass or plant had to be botanically correct – there was no excuse for inaccuracy.

He was an avid believer that there was no reason why bird illustrators should not introduce a *little art* into their work, and to prove his point, he undertook the enormous task of painting all the birds on the British list for Dr David Bannerman's book, when he was well into his eighties. The final volumes were not published until after his death, but they remain as a monument to his work as a bird painter.

Lodge had a great sense of humour and gave me much advice all of which I have tried to heed. He once told me to believe only a quarter of what I heard and half of what I saw. He then said that he had found a black grouse on the outskirts of Camberley, which was a very, very unlikely place to find one. He warned me, 'Never date your pictures, visitors to your studio always want to buy the one you did yesterday not two years ago.' When I spotted a picture which he had dated, the juvenile plumage of a gyr falcon *(Bannerman & Lodge Vol 5)*, he said with a smile, 'When you are ninety-two you can.' On another occasion he said a man had written to him saying he had just bought two old paintings of his done on wooden panels what should he do with them? Lodge chuckled, 'I told him to burn them at once.' On another visit to his studio he hailed me with the words, 'What a pity you didn't come to tea yesterday when I had another chap who, like you, had been in the Army. 'Yes' he went on 'a fellow called Alanbrooke,' (Lord Alanbrooke was a Field Marshal; I a very junior officer) when he was well into his eighties.

Tempera & Gouache

Lodge's pictures are always distinctive and easily recognisable by the way he painted backgrounds; the vegetation and rocks were always very much part of the picture and never tediously overworked. His colours were invariably soft and kind to the eye. Although he produced a number of large oil paintings much of his best work was done in tempera, but as eggs could not be used for this purpose during the war years he resorted to gouache, often painting on brown paper. He encouraged me to continue painting in gouache and showed me how he used old shaving brushes to smooth out clouds. 'Most people' he said 'find tempera far too difficult a medium and soon give up using it.'

For me the great thing about George Edward Lodge was his tremendous enthusiasm, which never diminished despite his age, and the unstinted help he gave to all those who sought it, and like me, sat at his feet.

Dick Treleaven
G.E.L. Trust Trustee

Dick Treleaven M.B.E. in his studio.

Background

The Chairman's Introduction...

This book is the first to be published by the George Edward Lodge Trust. The Trust hopes you enjoy the content and find it of merit. There are larger G.E. Lodge publications being planned for the future, especially on falconry and raptors.

The newly formed Trust was established in 2007 to advance education of the public in the artwork, life and skills of G.E. Lodge. One of the Trust's activities is to build an historical picture of falconry in the 19th and early 20th centuries based particularly upon his artwork, records and diaries. It therefore, seems only appropriate that the Trust begins with George Lodge's initial introduction to the art of falconry, and his earliest illustrations which appear in 'MODERN FALCONRY', an article written by E.B. Michell. The original article is reproduced on the following pages. 'MODERN FALCONRY' was commissioned for *The English Illustrated Magazine, 1885-1886*, and published by Macmillan and Co, London and New York.

The illustrations for this early work are from wood-engravings, and you will notice at the bottom of each illustration that he has signed 'G.E. Lodge del. et sc.' This signifies that he had both drawn (delineavit) and engraved (sculpsit) these wood blocks. Lodge's engravings capture the spirit of the sport and are of great interest to falconer's and sportsman alike.

I can do no better than let George Lodge the artist himself explain in his introduction how this work transpired.

Brian Bird
G.E.L. Trust Chairman, and Falconer

Brian Bird, rook-hawking on Salisbury Plain.

Introduction

From George Lodge's notes

'My first introduction to the noble sport of falconry was in this wise. In 1885, Messrs Macmillan, being the publishers of the English Illustrated Magazine, commissioned me to draw and engrave on wood the illustrations for an article on falconry, which was to be written by E.B. Michell. As I had never seen at that time anything of hawking, they gave me an introduction to Michell, so as to talk things over and see what could be done about it. Michell very wisely came to the conclusion that I ought, if possible, to see something of the sport before embarking on these illustrations; and he presently remembered that he had passed on to Mr T.J. Mann a nest of eyass merlins. The result was a most cordial invitation for us both to go down and stay for a few days with him at Bishop's Stortford, and see what sport we could with the merlins, and also see peregrines in training, flying to the lure. Thus started a friendship which lasted a lifetime.'

August. 21. 1885.

Went to Bishop's Stortford for some hawking with T.J. Mann's merlins. We had 2 or 3 flights in afternoon, and 1 kill.

August. 22. 1885.

Michell (E.B.) came, had some good flights with 2 cast merlins, 3 kills (1 double), 2 put in and taken, 1 put in and lost. The female merlins scored the kills, flew them in casts, the females together, and the jacks together. Mann has 3 casts of merlins (1 cast in moult), also a cast of falcons, and cast of tiercels.

Merlin 'feeding up'. Pen and wash drawing by G.E. Lodge.

George Edward Lodge
1860-1954

George Lodge – a portrait of an artist, in his Camberley studio 1947.

George Edward Lodge wildlife artist, naturalist and falconer, was born at Horncastle in Lincolnshire. An accomplished taxidermist, beginning with his first subject, an owl, at the age of twelve, he was also a foremost authority on birds of prey and unquestionably at his best when painting these subjects. George Lodge had been an active member of the Old Hawking Club at their meetings on Salisbury Plain as early as 1890.

A great sportsman, he particularly enjoyed his annual visits to Scotland and to the salmon rivers of Norway, from which countries he gathered much material for his work on raptors.

He was also a prolific illustrator, best remembered for his superb illustrations for Dr Bannerman's twelve volumes of 'The Birds of the British Isles'.

Edward Blair Michell
1842-1926

E.B. Michell – with one of his beloved merlins.

Edward Blair Michell of Wyke Champflower, Bruton, Somerset was a barrister, author, great sportsman, and probably the greatest living authority at that time on the merlin falcon.

He was at one time legal adviser to the King of Siam and in earlier years had been a fine athlete, and held many trophies in boxing, sculling and walking.

As the oldest living falconer of distinction he was often known as 'The father of falconry.' His classic book – *'The Art and Practice of Hawking'*, published 1900, is still recognised as one of the leading works on the subject.

MODERN FALCONRY

An article from

The English Illustrated Magazine
1885-1886

Illustrations
George E. Lodge

Author
E.B. Michell

ROOK HAWKING.
From a Drawing by GEORGE E. LODGE.

MODERN FALCONRY.

ALTHOUGH the art and practice of falconry have long gone out of fashion in these islands, it is quite a mistake to suppose that the old sport has ever become extinct. The falconers of to-day, both amateur and professional, are successors in a direct line of those who in a distant age claimed to hold their heads as high as any leader of the chase. It is true that at times the line has nearly been broken, and it has seemed as if nothing could save the art from becoming lost; but during the two centuries which have now almost elapsed since gun and cartridges usurped the place formerly occupied by hood and leash, there has never ceased to be a sprinkling of men, both gentle and simple, who have taken a pride and pleasure in their trained falcons and hawks.

That little should have been heard or known of these stubborn votaries of an un-fashionable sport is no surprising matter. Little is now known or heard of the falconers who nevertheless survive in various parts of England, Scotland, and Ireland. They neither have, nor wish to have, any chronicler. They console themselves easily for the absence of any loquacious reporter to describe their

doings in the style which we know so well in accounts of a long day with the Pytchley or a fast run with the Quorn. Their operations are carried on of necessity in remote and solitary districts, where jealous game-pre-servers or interloping cockneys have the least chance of interfering to spoil their plans. It is very difficult for any chance stranger to procure even a sight of a trained hawk, and still more hopeless to think of getting out to see one flown. It may there-fore be all the more interesting to explain to the uninitiated some of the mysteries of this occult art, and exhibit for their benefit some of the *dramatis personæ*, by whose aid it is practised.

The noble bird which is represented on page 656 belongs to the family of falcons which was most highly esteemed by the old falconers. Naturalists call it the gyr-falcon, and for a long time believed that it was one of those species which assume a different plumage according to the part of the world in which they are found. The better opinion now seems to be that there are three distinct species, all owning the common appellation of *gyr*— which is derived probably from the *gyrations* they describe in the air, just as the Greek name for a falcon signified the "circling" bird—but also having each a special distinctive name. The commonest of these three is the Norway falcon, which is somewhat smaller than the others and of a darker colour, often in its first year as dark as a peregrine. Next comes the Iceland falcon, which is of a much lighter hue and a more robust make, with a longer expanse of wing in proportion to its length. Third and largest of all is the Greenland falcon, represented in our illustration, which, although it is almost as brown as a peregrine in its first year, becomes gradually lighter until after many moults it appears almost of a pure white. The last spot where the dark brown disappears is the end of the long wing feathers where they cross over the upper part of the tail.

The reasons for believing that the Norway "gyr" differs from its congeners which inhabit the Arctic Circle depend not alone upon the difference in the markings. It is known that the ancient falconers paid higher sums for the Icelanders than for those from the mainland; and when the King of Denmark sent, as he often did, a complimentary present to some other potentate, he always sent to Iceland for them, and not to the neighbouring mountains of Norway. The courage of the more northern bird was admitted to be greater, and its style was also regarded as more grand—a very great point, as we shall see, in estimating the worth of a hawk. Nor was this all; the very character of the two species—for the Greenland falcon was hardly known then — showed a decided variance, and made it necessary to set about the training of the two species on a somewhat different system.

In our own times few gyr-falcons of either kind have been trained and flown in England. John Barr had some half-trained Norwegian gyrs near London about nine years ago, and a few years before that he had made a special journey to Iceland, and there trapped some Iceland falcons; but it does not appear that any one of these achieved great renown in this country. Within the last ten years the Old Hawking Club has had a gyr which flew rooks well; and Major Fisher also had one of which he expected great things at the same flight; but it died before it could be properly tried. On the whole, however, this sort of hawk has gone quite out of fashion. Some modern falconers declare that gyrs are not practically better than peregrines; and it is true that for the kind of flying now possible the peregrine is quite

good enough. The merit of the gyr, and especially of the Icelander and Greenlander, is that they will attack such powerful quarry as the crane, the wild goose, and the kite, which may be said to be beyond the power and strength of even the best peregrines. The advantage possessed by the larger falcon may be fairly estimated by comparing its size with that of the second on the list. The female gyr figured by Yarrell measured twenty-three inches from beak to tail, whereas very few female peregrines exceed eighteen inches. As the symmetry of the two species is almost identical, and the proportion of wing and tail power is about the same, it is reasonable to suppose that in weight and strength the gyr has an advantage of at least twenty per cent. The wing feathers of the latter seem, however, to be stouter in proportion to their length, while the whole frame appears rather more firmly set. Accordingly, although the difference in speed between them may not be great, it has always been observed that, in spite of its far greater weight and momentum, the gyr-falcon turns more quickly and easily than the other.

The peregrine—so called because it is found in almost all parts of the world, and migrates annually to unknown distances—is now *par excellence*, in England at least, the falconer's favourite. The illustration shows two of these beautiful birds standing on one of the perches which are commonly occupied by trained hawks when they are indoors. The bird on the right hand, wearing a hood, is a male or tiercel, and will be seen to be, as his name implies, about one-third less in size than the falcon beside him. The markings on his breast and flanks running transversely and not longitudinally, show him to be in the adult plumage, or in other words, to have gone through at least one moult; and the fact that these markings grow very faint on the upper part of the throat, fading away into an almost perfect white, show that a good many of these changes of plumage have been made. This is indeed the representation of a tried and valued servant of one of our most skilful falconers—a game hawk which has been flown for several seasons, and has a long score of partridges as well as some half-dozen grouse standing to his credit in the game register. The larger bird which stands unhooded on the left is a female peregrine, or "falcon," technically so called in contradistinction to the tiercel. She has only lately been caught and reclaimed, and is still in the immature plumage, with dark chocolate-coloured feathers on the back, and streaks of brown passing down her breast longitudinally. On the left leg of each of these, hidden beneath the feathers, is a small brass bell like that which they use on bicycles, but much finer and lighter, and on each of their legs is a " jess," or strap of thin leather, neatly fastened round it. The ends of each pair of jesses are attached by slits in them to a brass swivel made in the form of a figure 8 ; and through the further end of this swivel is passed the leash by which it is firmly tied down to the perch by means of a "falconer's knot." By rights the perch should have close underneath it a screen of canvas hanging down, by which the hawks, if they jump off, may climb up again ; but as this would have rather interfered with the full view of the bird's feathers it has been omitted in the sketch. For a similar reason the two birds are represented as standing closer together than they would be on a real perch, where care is taken to keep each out of arm's reach—or rather out of leg's reach of his or her neighbour.

How do they come to be standing so quietly there, as if nothing could be more natural and agreeable to them? To describe the whole process whereby this effect is produced—whereby their natural wildness and fierceness are subdued, and they are reconciled to captivity and to the presence of man—would lead us rather too far. The training of hawks is a business in itself. In the old days every well-born and well-bred countryman went through a long apprenticeship to it. Seldom, even then, was a man an adept at managing more than one kind of hawk. He will be clever, now, if he thoroughly understands even one kind of flight. Men who have for years kept and flown hawks in this country readily admit that they have still a great deal to learn, and are not above picking up a hint from their Oriental *confrères*. But it may be explained that there are two different classes of peregrines commonly used for the chase, of which the two birds figured above are representatives. The first is the "haggard" or "passage" falcon, caught after it has for some months or years found its own living ; and the other is the "eyess" or "nestling," taken from the nest before it can well fly, and brought up from that time under the eye of its master. There are, of course, "passage falcons," and "passage tiercels," according to the sex ; but, as it happens, the demand for the latter has now almost died out. And there are in like manner eyess tiercels and eyess falcons, which are now in about equal request. A few words must

suffice to explain the several methods of procuring and training these birds.

Passage peregrines are caught regularly, while on the autumn passage, by Dutch falconers, who lie in wait for them on the broad open plain of Valkenswaard, where for many long centuries the same elaborate devices have been employed for a like purpose. Old Adrien Mollen and his sons sit ensconced in concealed huts on the plain, luring down the migratory hawks, whose approach is notified to them by a tame butcher-bird kept on a perch close by. There come down to the lures annually some twenty or thirty peregrines, a few merlins, and an occasional goshawk, besides some few of the baser sort of hawks, as buzzards and harriers. The tiercels which are taken are usually all set free again, for there are, as already mentioned, few purchasers for them. The falcons are all kept, unless indeed, as sometimes is the case, the purchasers insist upon having only young birds. The present fashion is to use in preference for rook-hawking, the "red" falcons—in their first year's plumage. "Haggards," in the "blue," or adult plumage, are said to range too wide and give too much trouble. Consequently it is sometimes necessary to liberate also some of the old passage falcons as well as the tiercels. But all red falcons are carefully kept, and so usually are the merlins and goshawks, for whom it is pretty easy to find owners. Occasionally a wild peregrine is caught in England. One was taken early last autumn on the Plain by a well-known falconer, and is now in training. But however the passage hawk is obtained, it is dealt with in much the same manner. It is hooded and kept very quiet till the first wildness has worn off ; then handled skilfully and gently, and taught to know its owner ; next made to come to the lure for food ; and lastly, taught to "wait on" in the air around the falconer. When thus "reclaimed" it is ready to be flown at the quarry intended for it. The passage hawks caught in November are ready by the early spring, and should be flying rooks in February, or at least in the beginning of March.

Just such a falcon is "Lady Jane," above represented. Let us follow her fortunes for a day in March, and see how she acquits herself on the bleak expanse of Salisbury Plain, where perhaps the best rook-hawking in the world is now to be had. Early in the morning she will have been taken from the screen-perch on which she passed the night, and fastened by the leash to the ring of the block which stands in the paddock outside.

GREENLAND GYR-FALCON.
From a Drawing by GEORGE E. LODGE.

G.E.Lodge. del et Sc

By falconers this is termed "weathering." There she will sit pluming herself and ruffling her feathers, looking now at the distant clouds, or at some passing bird too far off to be seen by human eye, and now at her companions, who sit on each side of her on similar blocks. About eleven o'clock she will be called to the fist of the falconer, and by him hooded and placed on one side of a "cadge," or else in the "van." A cadge is a sort of light frame which one sees in hawking pictures, or in a representation of *As You Like It* on the stage. On its padded sides are tied several hooded hawks—six or eight, perhaps—and in the middle of this walks the falconer's man, anciently called the "cadger," carrying the whole affair by means of straps crossed over his shoulders. The van is a more elaborate structure—a sort of omnibus with perches inside, drawn by a horse or a pair of horses, and forming a much more comfortable place for the occupants, as it shelters them from the bitter wind as well as the rain and sun.

But when "Lady Jane's" turn comes to fly, she is taken from her place, whether on cadge or in van, on to the fist of her master, who rides off straightway to the place where a rook is known or expected to be. Her leash is taken off; the swivel which attached it to the jesses is removed from them, and their ends are grasped between the fingers and thumb of the man who is to let her go. Moreover, that there may be no

LARK-HAWKING, ADULT MALE MERLINS.
From a Drawing by GEORGE E. LODGE.

delay at the critical moment, the straps of her hood behind are drawn, so as to loosen it, and enable it to be pulled off at any moment. Thus everything is ready as the falconer rides along at a smart pace holding his gauntleted left hand as steady as he can, and keeping his weather eye open for any rook that may come towards him down the wind, or pass on the windward side. No rook must ever be flown when he is to leeward of the hawk; a hundred yards' start that way is a greater advantage to him than half a mile in the other direction. But suppose one to pass obliquely across about a quarter of a mile up wind? Just as he crosses the exact line in which the wind blows towards "Lady Jane," her hood is

U U

pulled off, the falconer's arm is raised, and with a short whoop of encouragement she is "cast off" at the quarry. There is very little delay at the start. If the wind is very high the falcon will perhaps swerve a bit to the right or left. But in a second more she steadies herself, and with a single glance at the rook, begins to "mount" towards him in a long slanting line.

It is amazing how quickly both the pursuer and the pursued know "what is up." An old cock rook, who, like his younger relatives, is in the prime of condition in February and March, will begin climbing up into the sky as quickly as the falcon

is from that height, after a long, long climb upwards, that she comes down in a steep descent, not flying, nor yet falling like an inanimate mass, but gliding downwards obliquely, with wings half-closed and tail compressed. As she nears the rook he also swoops about in a strange manner, wriggling, as it were, in his flight so as to baffle the pursuer; and in nine cases out of ten he succeeds in his purpose. It is far more difficult, of course, for a hawk to strike a bird in the free air than for a greyhound to pick up a hare on the flat surface of the ground. The impetus of the falcon falling from a height above gives her, it is true, plenty of speed to overtake her quarry, but

CAST OF MERLINS—IMMATURE PLUMAGE.
From a Drawing by GEORGE E. LODGE.

behind him, and if he has had a good start, may go up some hundreds of feet before the enemy approaches. From a bad peregrine—from many of the eyesses, for instance, and from every peregrine that is badly trained, or insufficiently fed—such a rook will fly away altogether, without a single "stoop" being made at him. But "Lady Jane" is a fast hawk. Before she was caught in Holland she had struck down many a wild duck, and even a few big gulls, which are ever so much stronger on the wing than any rook. She goes for the quarry in masterly style, not making straight for him at all, but going in a line which takes her wide of him, and far higher in the air. It

it makes the steering very difficult; and however keen her sight and quick her turns, she seldom does more at the first attempt than brush close past the wriggling body of the rook. But then, having missed, she shoots up, if she is a good hawk, instantly, utilising the last remains of her impetus. Sometimes this shoot upwards takes her fifty feet or more above the place where she passed the fugitive, and after a few beats of her wings, to bring her into convenient position, she is ready to be at him again. Sometimes when the rook is clever and has made a good shift from the first stoop, a long climb has again to be made, and before a second stoop can be made, the two birds are many hundred yards away from the scene of their first encounter. But throughout the flight, however long, there is a repetition of the same tactics—mounting on the part of both till a stoop can be made, and then a trial of skill very much resembling that between the hare and the greyhound. Some flights are quickly over, in others there will be perhaps a dozen stoops or more, and the space traversed will be a mile or more as the crow flies, but three times that distance reckoning in the *détours* made by the principal performers. Often, if the country is at all enclosed, the rook will make good his escape to cover, and from the safe shelter of a belt of firs, or even a single tree, bid defiance to the falcon and to the whole company of mounted men who follow behind. If the tree is tall, it is seldom possible to dislodge the fugitive. Even climbing into the branches is of little avail, for the old rook will shift from twig to twig, and altogether decline to go out into the open while the falcon is wheeling about in the air overhead. But if no cover be near, and the peregrine is in good wind and fettle, there comes at length the moment when a stoop, more deadly and well directed than those before it, brings the two flying bodies together. The sharp talons which lie hidden underneath the falcon's white feathers come into contact with the wing, back, or neck of the fugitive, and either catch there, or else tearing through the flesh, topple the victim over. In rook-hawking, the falcon having once caught hold seldom lets go again : the helpless body of the rook is dragged along by the victorious foe, and both descend to the ground, where a few seconds suffice for the peregrine to despatch her quarry.

There are two other flights for which this kind of hawk is commonly used. The more characteristic of these is game - hawking, which by many good falconers is preferred to the sport with rooks. But as it is followed at quite a different time of year there is no reason why the same men should not be fond of both ; and indeed many of the peregrines which do duty on the plain in March are found distinguishing themselves equally on the moors in the following August and September. But though the same hawk may be employed, her tactics must be very different. When grouse are the quarry a first-rate pointer or setter should be employed. When the dog comes to a point, the peregrine is unhooded and thrown off, and she mounts in easy circles to a considerable height above him. Then the birds are flushed, and "Lady Jane," "towering in her pride of

place," comes down like a thunderbolt behind them, sweeping with tremendous speed through the fast-flying pack, and either striking one down as she passes, or "throwing up" again instantly for another stoop. In this business the stoop is much grander, for the falcon falls headlong almost like a stone from her great height, and the force of the stroke is such as often to break the back or even sever the head of the unlucky victim. Falcons are most used for this sport, and occasionally, though not often, the " eyesses " prove as good at it as the more practised " haggards." They are moreover generally to be flown with less risk, for when the haggard is aloft, perhaps half a mile high, there is a great temptation to her to start in pursuit of some distant quarry—a passing rook or wood pigeon—instead of patiently " waiting on " in attendance upon the dog and men below.

For partridge-hawking tiercels are good enough, and the manner of flight is the same. Eyesses are most often used, and these will often continue to improve not only during their first season, but during several years after they have been moulted in captivity. The " blue " tiercel in our engraving is one that has so been moulted. He came from Lundy Island—a famous eyrie—and is called " Lundy," one of the best hawks that ever flew at game. No fear when he is thrown off in a big field of swedes that he will " rake away " after vain pursuits. Well he knows the sight of the dog standing motionless at the point ; well he knows that if he is to have a chance to cut down his partridge before it reaches the hedge, he must mount high into the clouds, and keep a little to windward of the pointer. Very deadly is his first stoop, which he knows is the most formidable. And he is tamer than a parrot withal, never moved in the spirit to carry off his slain quarry, or to object to being taken from it by the falconer and hooded ready for another flight.

Magpie-hawking is a sort of combination of these two different kinds of flight. It is a favourite sport in Ireland, and affords an immense amount of exercise to the followers on foot. That cunning knave " mag " is found in some bush or spinney, dislodged therefrom with shouts and whips, and at once pursued by a tiercel or two. If not cut down at the first stoop, he will soon be back to some spinney, or tree, or hedge, and thence the whole company must drive him, somehow or other, while the hawks "wait on" in circles over the spot. A deal of patience

CAST OF PEREGRINES—RED FALCON AND BLUE TIERCEL.
From a Drawing by GEORGE E. LODGE.

and some considerable strength of wing is required on the part of the hawk to enable him to keep his position in the air so long. Meanwhile the task of the pedestrian is neither light nor short. A dozen times the shifty quarry will sneak back to some friendly shelter, and as many times will the hawking party with whoops and cracking of whips have to force him back into the open again.

We come now to a different kind of hawk—the smallest of all the English falcons. The female merlin is only about twelve inches long; the male or "Jack," only ten—exactly the same length as a big blackbird. Yet both these little creatures have occasionally been trained to take young partridges; the females have been known to fly at magpies, and will readily take large pigeons. A great deal of sport may be had with either of them at blackbirds and thrushes, which they will pursue in the same way as sparrow-hawks. But the flight *par excellence* of the merlin is at skylarks; and this alone is worth a special description. It is an almost perfect copy of the old flight at herons, save that it lacks the very doubtful attraction of a fight on the ground to follow. The merlin, or the pair of merlins, whether male or female, whether eyess or wild-caught, are taken un-hooded into the field, and a lark is walked up, after which both start like lightning from the fist. Then ensues a long climb upwards into the air, the lark mounting in small circles, and the falcons in larger rings, either from right to left or from left to right, as chance ordains. When the hawks are close to their quarry they stoop at it like peregrines, one backing up the stoop of her fellow by a second one. Many a good lark will run the gauntlet of thirty such stoops and get off safe to cover. Sometimes the lark will mount up in a clear sky till he is altogether out of sight, and from thence be brought down yard after yard by the fierce attacks of his little enemies. The twists and turns of these small birds are much more swift and active than those of the peregrine and rook, and what the flight of the merlin loses in grandeur when compared with that of the big falcons, it is often thought to gain by its neatness and extreme rapidity. Here everything is on so small a scale that the flight can often be followed on foot, and the little hawks seen stooping and recovering themselves within a few feet of the spec-

SPARROWHAWK AND BLACKBIRD.
From a Drawing by GEORGE E. LODGE.

tator, as shown in the illustration. Eyesses have been known to fly a dozen larks each in one day, and kill four or five of them. But the most deadly performer is an old male such as "Peter" above represented, who, as he "throws up" after an unsuccessful stoop, shows the splendid markings of his blue plumage in which, before he was snared, he struck down many a winter lark, and perhaps even some snipe and youthful swallows.

Merlins are almost absurdly tame and easy to train, but they are deeply addicted to the vice of "carrying," or, in other words, bolting with their quarry. The only remedy for this is to make complete pets of them, feeding them together on the fist, as in a foregoing illustration, whenever there is an opportunity after they have finished their day's work and are engaged in a friendly meal upon the lark which they have together pursued into the sky. These youngsters—only three months old—have exactly similar markings, and differ only in size, the male being about one-sixth smaller than the female. But the adult male, with his slatey-blue back and broad black bar at the end of the tail, is almost as unlike what he was in the chocolate-coloured plumage of his youth as a wood-pigeon is to a partridge.

Thus far we have spoken only of the nobler race of birds of prey—the "falcons," properly so-called, or "long-winged" species, the tips of whose wings when folded as the bird is at rest cross one another above the tail, and reach almost to the end of the tail-feathers. The other sort—the "short-winged" hawks—are, as the name implies, distinguished by their shorter and more rounded wings, longer tail, and by the colour of the eyes, which are yellow instead of the dark hazel-brown of the falcons. But their style and manner of flying is altogether differ- ent, and so is also their character and the manner of training them. In this class are includ- ed, as far as the falconer is

RABBIT HAWKING—ADULT GOSHAWK.
From a Drawing by GEORGE E. LODGE.

concerned with it, only two species—the goshawk and the sparrow-hawk—but each of these has its own very distinct quarry to pursue, proportioned duly to its size and strength. As the sparrow-hawk is still a common bird in England, and can often be procured, it may be well to describe it first, although by reason of its queer temper there are few amateurs who will be at the pains to train it.

The best sparrow-hawks are those which have been caught wild; and one may be not unfrequently picked up from a bird-catcher, into whose nets it has come after one of his call-birds. For several days and nights consecutively the captive must be kept awake on the glove of its master or an assistant, and for many a day it must feed there only, and be taught gradually to come longer and longer distances to the fist for food. Indeed, the short-winged hawk, according to a maxim of the old falconers, " should know no perch but its master's fist." The more it is carried on the hand and talked to and stroked with a feather, and

who deservedly think a great deal of this hawk, and make a large use of it for taking quail, carry it bodily in their hand, grasping it round the middle, and, as the quarry gets up, throw it at them like a hand-grenade; and it is said that the hawks very soon become accustomed to this practice, and rather enjoy the fun than otherwise. But the more common objects of pursuit, even with female sparrow-hawks, are the larger hedgerow birds—thrushes, blackbirds, and an occasional redwing or missel thrush. When these can be walked up in a large field of swedes or turnips, as is often the case in September, a good open flight is certain, and a kill very likely indeed; but when the hedges have to be beaten, the pursuit becomes very like magpie-hawking, with this exception, that the hawk, instead of waiting on above, returns to the fist and remains there, waiting in the utmost excitement for the fugitive to be driven out. Moreover, the latter must choose a very thick spot in the hedge to creep into for safety,

GOSHAWK ON BOW PERCH (IMMATURE PLUMAGE).
From a Drawing by GEORGE E. LODGE.

fed with small pieces on the end of the finger, the sooner will it put off the Old Adam of fierceness and suspicion, and begin to come readily to the master when called. As soon as this desirable stage has been reached, the hawk may be taken into the field and flown at a suitable quarry. The female sparrow-hawk, which is about fifteen inches long, is often strong enough to take partridges, but must have a good start, or she will not have sufficient speed to overtake them. There is, of course, no chance of making any short-winged hawk " wait on " in the air above. She must be thrown off at the bird as it rises, in the same way as described in rook-hawking or lark-hawking. The Oriental falconers, indeed,

or his pursuer will come after him, and, plunging headlong into the thicket, drag him forth from his hiding-place. One of our illustrations shows a blackbird darting into cover with the sparrow-hawk close behind, swooping over the top of the hedge just too late to catch him before he reaches a safe thicket of thorns.

The male sparrow-hawk, or "musket" as he used to be called, is a very much smaller bird, but slimmer looking and perhaps rather better proportioned than his sisters. Some individuals are very tiny indeed, and with their thin long legs and slender feet look quite like miniature hawks. Their character is also usually less sulky and unmanageable. It is a pity that more beginners do not try their hand at this sort of hawk. The difficulty is that they are extremely delicate—perhaps even more so than merlins—and liable, if the least mistake is made, to be attacked with cramp in the legs. There is, however, no doubt that in the old times many a cheery afternoon was spent by the yeoman and his friends beating the hedgerows for small birds with no other companions than a few sparrow-hawks. And now that the country is so much enclosed, this sort of hawk would be still more handy in most parts of England. But why lament over the bygone glories of "birding," as Shakespeare calls it? Is there not to this day an enthusiastic squire in Herefordshire who flies his impetuous little "Blanche" at blackbirds with as much ardour and success as his mediæval ancestors?

The last, but in many respects the most valuable, of our feathered friends, is the goshawk —a large, powerful creature, having a body somewhat larger than a peregrine, but with a much longer tail. This hawk is of far stronger build than the sparrow-hawk, especially in the legs and feet, which are large, thick, and armed with immense claws as sharp as needles. The manner of training and flying the goshawk is like that employed for the sparrow-hawk. She returns to the fist after unsuccessful flights, and not, as falcons do, to the "lure." A powerful female is good enough to take hares; and there is a gallant falconer now living whose "Agrippa" has rolled over many such honourable quarry. But for the rank and file of female goshawks rabbits are the usual game, and very exciting it is to see the determined stoops of the bird and the sharp turns of the quadruped as it shifts from the stroke. To strike the quarry and bowl it over is not all that is required; a still more difficult task is often the holding on to so vigorous an enemy. Rabbit-hawking is the nearest approach which we can make in this country to those favourite Oriental sports such as the pursuit of deer and foxes with eagles, or gazelles with the saker. A male goshawk might be flown with great success at pheasants, or at partridges when they are not too wild; and he will work admirably with a few spaniels as allies to help him in putting out the birds which he has driven into cover.

These short-winged hawks, when pegged out on the lawn, are usually made to stand on bow-perches, made of arched wood, as in a previous illustration, and not on solid blocks like the falcons. They like, as it seems, to keep their strong toes grasping a round substance, and to spread their long, fan-shaped tails out under

THE FALCONER.
From a Drawing by GEORGE E. LODGE.

them as they face the wind. The modern practice is not to keep the short-winged hawks hooded except when travelling about, but it seems probable that in early times hoods were worn a good deal more. These hawks have a tendency, when left unused for a while, to become quite dull and sluggish, and then need a deal of carrying on the fist to bring them into fettle again. Their bells are attached, not to the feet, as in the case of falcons, but to the central feathers of the tail, which, as it is almost constantly in motion, even when the hawk is sitting still, affords a better indication of their whereabouts than the other plan.

A falconer who has the exclusive care of half a dozen trained birds, whether falcons or hawks, or both, finds little time hanging heavily on his hands. By the time he has moved out his charges to the lawn and set their nocturnal abode in order, he will have got an appetite for his own breakfast. Then there is the business of feeding those hawks which are not to fly, and perhaps exercising most of them to the lure, in the manner so graphically described by Izaac Walton. Then the bath or baths must be filled, and the hawks which are to be indulged with that luxury moved to a place where they can jump in and splash about to their hearts' delight. Then the plan of the day's campaign must be arranged, having regard to wind and weather, and the chance of where the quarry is most likely to be found; and when the day's work in the field is over the falconer's day is not nearly done. There is the "feeding up" of the hawks that have not been allowed, or have not had time, to "take their pleasure" on the quarry. Everything depends upon meting out to the hungry creatures just that quantity of food which will keep them in full health and strength, but without over-gorging them or making them inactive on the morrow. If a feather has been broken by some accident during the day it must be mended at once; if a jess is worn out it must be replaced. The feet and beaks of all the hawks should be cleansed, their hoods seen to, and the lures made ready for use on another day. Nor let it be forgotten that there is such a thing as losing a hawk. When this disaster happens the country is scoured till dark in search of the truant, and, if not found, the falconer, before break of day, is again on the look-out with his lure in hand. A successful falconer lies on no bed of roses. Only constant attention will make his hawks fond of him. But when they are so, he stands amongst them a friend amongst faithful friends. At a sign from him they will jump towards him; nay, at his first appearance—in the words of the old sportsman—they "rejoyce." The character of each of them—for hawks differ in character as much as men and women—is as well known to him as his own. He knows what can or cannot be done with each; and thus he is still able to carry on the most difficult of all sports without the disappointments that have frightened away from it less patient and persevering tyros.

E. B. MICHELL.

Falconry by Gilbert Blaine

Published by Philip Allan, London 1936

From George Lodge's notes (Book Review)

The name of the author of this notable addition to the "Sportsman's Library" is a sufficient guarantee of the excellence of the contents. An enthusiastic falconer of 40 years experience, with the means and leisure to pursue this most fascinating and exacting sport to his heart's desire, he has put into words for the use of those who are able to follow in his footsteps, the results of all those years of experience, and the methods by means of which those results were obtained. One of the chief merits of the book is its concise brevity the extraordinary amount of detailed information being given in such clear language in such a short space of pages. And it must be remembered that every word of it is first hand practical knowledge, and such being the case, the bulk of the book is taken up with the art of training the Peregrine, of which species, and the sport to be obtained in this particular branch of falconry. He is such a devotee that he has comparatively little to say about the other branches of the sport, although there are extremely useful chapters on the training and management of Goshawks, Sparrowhawks, and Merlins.

He wastes no time in elaborate descriptions of the plumages of the various species of hawks, such can be obtained from books on Ornithology, but gets straight to work at the subject in view, and the result is a most masterly and comprehensive account of the whole elaborate process of training and management of hawks – from the taking of eyasses from the eyrie to the final triumph of killing wild quarry with them. Step by step, every stage is described in full detail, hacking, manning, training to fly to the lure, entering to quarry, and ultimately flying at wild quarry, with a wealth of safe instructions, and a grasp of the necessity of attending to every little detail, that makes it one of the most thorough books on the subject that has ever been written.

He is enthusiastically in favour of the passage hawk as compared with the eyass, in which opinion doubtless all falconers will agree, as having had the chance of knowing so much more during her life of freedom than the latter, just as the haggard may know just a bit too much, and so is a more risky subject for training, and is much more liable to be lost. As far as passage hawks are concerned, no doubt they are, as a rule, much superior to eyasses, although some of the authors own eyasses, especially some of his Lundy tiercels, have flown as high, waited on as steadily, and killed their quarry, grouse and partridges, as surely and regularly, as any passage tiercel that was ever flown. But, as he says, passage hawks, nowadays, are not obtainable, except by a fortuitous chance, and so eyasses alone must be made the best of, and a very good "best" that may be, in capable hands.

Haggards he dismisses in a few words. Doubtless they may be magnificent fliers, but are much more likely to be lost, owing to their longer experience of wild freedom. Gyr falcons are also dismissed with a few words. They have been tried at wild geese, but proved to be wanting in pluck when it came to driving home their stoop. They would doubtless take old Blackcocks, but on open fairly flat country would have to be chosen, and the falconer would have to be a very good athlete to follow and to help his hawk at the finish. A shifty old rook would probably beat any Gyr, except perhaps a very active tiercel.

Hobbies again are only mentioned as a species, and nothing said about training them. But in modern times nobody has been able to do anything with them in the shape of taking wild quarry, and probably they never were of any use except to fly to the lure, and to scare larks sufficiently to make them lie until they were netted. In a practical book on falconry, as is the one under review, it would serve no purpose taking up space on their behalf.

There is a short, but very adequate chapter on merlins and lark hawking, but it is to be doubted that any merlin that ever flew could catch a full grown snipe in fair flight. The ones that the wild merlin catch are probably young ones, or if old ones, taken on the ground. Two full grown snipe have been found at a nest of a pair of little owls, but no little owl could catch a snipe on the wing.

The North American "Coopers Hawk" is mentioned in the book as being probably a desirable bird to train for the purpose of flying partridges and pheasants. This would be an interesting experiment, and this hawk would probably take them quite well, being flown, like a goshawk, from the fist. The American Goshawk, too, might be tried, if only for the sake of comparing its capabilities and character with its European relative. This book, the result of so many years of first hand experience, is so good that it will hold its place in the highest ranks of the literature of British Field Sports.

So great is the author's insistence on the mastering of detail that he devotes a whole chapter to "Hooding", and gives it as his opinion that it takes a man two years before he can become an expert in hooding a falcon. Certain it is that some men never do become really expert in this dexterous manoeuvre. Elaborate instructions too are given as to the proper way of carrying a hawk on the fist, taking her from her block, or screen perch, putting her down again, tying the leash to the block or screen perch, and to many other matters.

The introductory chapter is very good, showing how and why falconry can never become again a popular sport, and showing also obstacles that beset the way of a beginner; and another excellent chapter on "A Plea for Falconry," in which, among other things he discusses the begged question as to whether the flying of hawks to game has the result of driving away the game from that particular moor or manor. It is true that some shooting people have a prejudice against hawking for this reason, and will go so far as to refuse to let their ground for hawking purposes; but the author is quite right in his conclusion that it does nothing of the sort, and that in fact the game is not so much disturbed or frightened as when the ground is shot over by a party of guns, either dogging or driving. Another chapter composed of 11 "Admonitions and Advice" will be found full of common sense, and more than that, it might be called "gentlemanly" sense, but no.8, admonition may be news to some, as it is to the writer of this review, which is to the effect that it is not well to stare at a hawk, and if she stares at you she must be humoured by you turning your eyes away.

The chapter on "Ailments and Remedies" shows the author to have more faith in some medicines than the majority of modern falconers have, these generally do not go further than prescribing "hot blood", or perchance 1/2 a rhubarb pill. But the author has evidently written from his personal experience, and doubtless has found these remedies efficacious. Blaine finished up this season (1913) with the excellent total of 406 grouse, 19 sundries. The score of the individual hawks being as follows:-

	Grouse	Sundries	Unsuccessful flights
Lundy III, eyass tiercel, 6 years old.	53	4	9
Gnome, passage tiercel, 4 years old.	41	9	12
Anna, eyass falcon, 1 year old.	51	-	19
Barbara, eyass falcon, 1 year old.	80	-	12
Sylvia, eyass falcon, young.	90	3	2
Nora, eyass falcon, young.	81	1	9
Gladys, passage falcon, 1 year old.	7	2	3
Another young eyass falcon.	3	-	1
Total	406	19	

This shows what can be done by an expert falconer with game hawks.

Peregrines on cadge. Pen and wash drawing by G.E. Lodge.

The Noble Art

From George Lodge's notes

It is good to know that at this present date, 1935, the noble art (for it is an art as well as a sport) of falconry has by means died out, rather, the reverse is the case; as there are a goodly number of young and enthusiastic devotees of the sport, even among members of some of our Public Schools; and there has also recently been formed the "British Falconers' Club." Most of the members of which, train and fly their own hawks, as the Club does not attain to the luxury of having a professional falconer attached to it, and many a head of quarry do they annex with their peregrines, goshawks, merlins and sparrowhawks. Rooks and crows are the quarry of the peregrines, as game hawking means renting a "shoot", and not only that, but in a suitable country for flying hawks at game, and in the whole length and breadth of the British Isles very few districts are at all suitable, the whole country being much too much enclosed. Wide open spaces with fences and trees few and far between being quite essential for any reasonable success – and for grouse hawking moors that are very fairly flat will be the only chance for a falconer to be able even to keep his hawk in sight during a flight.

Once over a skyline and the chances of a hawk being lost is very great; as not only has the direction of the flight been lost, but if a kill has taken place there is no knowing the distance it may be away, much less the direction and a hawk on its quarry among broken ground and heather is not to be seen unless it has been marked down when the kill takes place, and if it is a mile away – what then? She takes her pleasure on her quarry, and a long time at that, and afterwards flies off and sits on a stone for perhaps hours while she digests her meal, at such a time taking no notice of lures that she may see swinging a mile away, or anything else, and so another "lost hawk". When a hawk is lost, and left out all night, it is well to be in the neighbourhood at day break the next morning, when she may very likely be taken up, especially if another hawk is flown to the lure, when the lost hawk, if she is anywhere near, will be very liable to join in the flight, and so be taken down again all right.

Dutch hood. Pen and wash drawing by G.E. Lodge.

Paintings

George Edward Lodge has left behind an historical picture on falconry during the 19th and early 20th centuries. Some of the artwork in this publication is focused around Thomas Mann's hawking establishment. George Lodge recorded in his note books and hawking diary many hawking days with some of Mann's famous hawks, which he went on to sketch and paint. They now form an integral record for falconry heritage in the British Isles.

G.E.L. Trust

Trained merlin. Painting by G.E. Lodge.

Falconer with a goshawk. Painting by G.E. Lodge.

Thomas Mann's Rook Hawking Party

Thomas Mann's rook hawking party in Cambridgeshire, from an oil painting by G.E. Lodge in 1889. Thomas Mann stands by the cadge holding 'Vic', a peregrine falcon. Mann's professional falconer, Alfred Frost, kneels at the cadge. The two peregrines on the left of the cadge are 'Lady Salvin' and 'Lady Loch Vane', the property of Mann. A saker falcon is on the right of the cadge, property of R. Thompson. Lodge is seated on the ground, to the right, smoking his pipe. Both Mann and Lodge are wearing the green coats of the Old Hawking Club.

Tiercel moulting into blue plumage.

'Greenfoot', a hooded peregrine tiercel – gouache painting by G.E. Lodge.

The Falcon's Strike. Oil on canvas by G.E. Lodge.

Grouse Hawking

By George Edward Lodge

GROUSE hawking is the highest form of falconry in these days, the flight at the heron being entirely a thing of the past. First-rate dogs are necessary to find the grouse, and they should be very steady at the point, which may be some distance away. When thus found and the approach made, the falcon is cast off, and a halt made while she "makes her pitch." This done and she is steadily "waiting on" high overhead, the grouse must be flushed downwind so as to give the hawk her best chance in her stoop. Then will be felt the thrill of seeing a peregrine falcon in all the magnificence of her splendid powers and command of her energies. If she is very well placed, her stoop will be almost vertical, and if a good "footer" the quarry may be knocked down in a cloud of feathers, stone dead. But it often happens, indeed generally, that the grouse makes such pace that the hawk has to make a long, slanting stoop, coming down well behind the grouse and then rushes up and either knocks the grouse down or "trusses" it - which means catches it and carries it on a short distance before coming to ground with it.

The Falcon's Strike

A spaniel is a most useful adjunct on the moor with the hawks, in order to help flush a grouse after it has "put in" to some cover, long heather, bushes, etc., if the hawk has missed her stoop or been outflown by the grouse. Falcons always strike their quarry with their powerful hind talons. Immediately before striking the feet are thrust forward, so that having struck, there is sufficient play for the backward swing of the legs as the hawk rakes headlong forward over the object struck; otherwise she would break her legs with the shock of impact.

"Falcons" (female peregrines) are generally used for grouse, their weight being more fitted to cope with such strong quarry; the smaller "tiercels" (male peregrines) being more suitable for flying partridges, although I have seen tiercels as very good grouse hawks. Grouse lie very close when a peregrine is in the air, as the hawk always takes its quarry on the wing. But it is quite otherwise in the case of an eagle making its appearance. In this event, every grouse in the neighbourhood will take to the air and decamp at their best pace. Of course, they will return eventually; but many a grouse drive has been spoilt by the appearance of an eagle over the skyline. Hence the dislike of eagles by shooting men on a grouse moor. On the other hand, deer stalkers on deer forests encourage eagles which tend to keep down the hares and grouse that are liable to be a nuisance during a stalk. As their eyries are practically always on the high ground, this protective immunity enables them to hold their own; so that at the present time the golden eagle is not at all an uncommon bird in Scotland, and long may he remain so.

Extract from George Lodge's *Memoirs of an Artist Naturalist*

Half Albino Merlin

An abnormally coloured merlin came under my observations a few years ago. It was abnormal in two respects: first, it was half albino and second, what coloured plumage it had was the fully adult plumage of a male merlin, although it was a bird of the year and so had never moulted. It was taken from a nest in Yorkshire in which it was the only abnormally coloured one.

Another youngster in this nest had whitish-coloured claws. The bird came into the possession of Kim Muir, who let me have it for a week in order to take as many sketches as I wanted. I ultimately painted a life-sized portrait of it sitting on its block.

Peregrines weathering. Paintings by G.E. Lodge.

Extract from George Lodge's *Memoirs of an Artist Naturalist*

Hawks and Hawking

In the old days when I used to see a lot of rook hawking with the late T.J. Mann and his hawks in Cambridgeshire, we never used to slip the hawks at a flock of rooks if there were any jackdaws among them. Jackdaws are much more active than rooks, and if a hawk picks out a jackdaw instead of a rook she will never catch it, and may have such a long flight that a lot of time will be wasted before she is taken down. However, on one occasion I took up a lost hawk on a jackdaw she had killed, and on which I found her feeding. No one saw the flight so I do not know the manner of it, but it was about two miles downwind from where she had been slipped at a flock of rooks. That was in 1894.

The hawk herself was a passage falcon of the previous year, and a very good hawk. She gave many a fine exhibition of high-ringing flights. She was about the quickest one to get above rooks that I ever saw. On being thrown off at a rook, her tactics were immediately to take a long flight, either down or across wind close to the ground; then turning and throwing herself into the wind would come back, mounting at a tremendous pace, and would very soon be above the rooks. Being also a fine "stooper" and a good "footer," she generally killed her rook. Her name was *Stratagem*.

George Lodge painting 'Stratagem' at Hyde Hall, Sawbridgeworth, Hertfordshire, 1894.

'Stratagem', a peregrine on rook. Oil on canvas by G.E. Lodge. In 1894, she caught a total of 29 rooks and 1 jackdaw in 17 days.

Jack Mavrogordato's fine goshawk 'Helga' on a rabbit. She was flown during the 1930s. Painting by G.E. Lodge.

Peregrine falcon on grouse. Painting by G.E. Lodge.

Extract from George Lodge's *Diary of an Artist Falconer*

Shadow of Death

November. 21. 1889.

Sawbridgeworth, Herts. With Frost and "Shadow of Death". Round the hedgerows, but we got no kills. We only saw 4 rabbits, and they made the fences too quickly. One rabbit bolted out of the hedge, beyond Frost, and ran past him making back. Frost slipped the hawk when the rabbit was a direct crossing shot, and the rabbit made a most extraordinary leap as the hawk went at it. These things are done so quickly that it is very difficult for the eye to take in what really happens. But it appeared as if the rabbit jumped 3ft into the air, and clean over the hawk. He made the fence just in time to save himself, as the hawk had recovered herself very quickly, and went smash into the fence close behind the rabbit.

Sketches of 'Shadow of Death', a female goshawk. Pencil and wash by George Lodge. She was owned by T.J. Mann, and flown for seven seasons between 1886-1892.

'Shadow of Death', an oil painting by G.E. Lodge.

Peregrine falcon. Painting by G.E. Lodge.

American goshawk weathering. Painting by G.E. Lodge.

Adult goshawk weathering. Painting by G.E. Lodge.

Adult musket weathering. Painting by G.E. Lodge.

45

Falcons and Goshawk Weathering.

An illustration by George Lodge for 'The Art and Practice of Hawking,' 1900, written by E.B. Michell.

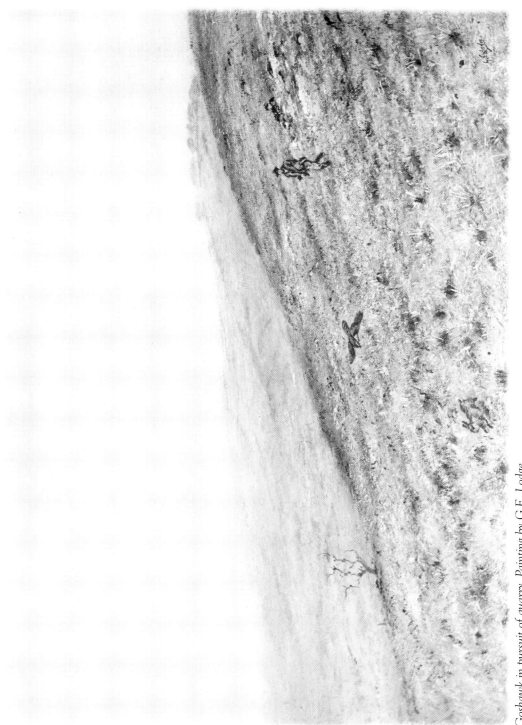

Goshawk in pursuit of quarry. Painting by G.E. Lodge.

Lodge the falconer, 1894.

Lodge the falconer, 1936.

Extract from George Lodge's *Memoirs of an Artist Naturalist*

Hawks and Hawking

The peregrine falcon (Falco peregrinus peregrinus Tunst.) is much commoner in this country than is generally supposed. It occurs frequently in autumn and winter in parts where it is rarely seen at other times, because northern-bred birds are then making their way south. These migrants often stay several weeks in a district where food, such as partridges and woodpigeons, is plentiful. The sea-cliffs of the British Isles provide many breeding sites, and so do the mountainous parts of Scotland and Wales.

Preservation of game has no doubt lessened the numbers of peregrine, but other factors such as the shrinking of areas on which desirable prey is present must also have played their part. There is little fear, anyway, that game preservation will cause the falcon to be exterminated, for it is well able to take care of itself, and the wilder parts of the country provide good sanctuary. I have many notes of having seen wild peregrines during days of shooting and hawking in Norfolk and Lincolnshire, where I have spent much of my time.

There seems to be a strong prejudice in some places against flying trained hawks over preserved ground, the argument being that the presence of the hawk tends to drive away permanently the existing stock of game, i.e. grouse and partridges. I think this idea is based more on fancy than fact. I have seen the same ground used for game hawking with peregrines for weeks at a time, flying the hawks at least three times each week and sometimes more, without any noticeable falling-off in the quantity of game.

When one comes to examine the facts, there seems little reason why game should leave. The peregrine is the natural enemy of game birds and they must often see wild peregrines - especially on the Scottish grouse moors. It does not frighten them unduly as long as they sit close until the hawk is out of sight. No one has ever heard of the presence of a wild falcon *denuding* a moor or a manor of game. It takes a variable toll, but the coveys will not leave the ground for such a reason. Their strong sense of home ground would not allow them to be so easily disturbed. After all, the upset from hawking is nothing like so great as when the birds are being driven over guns.

In hawking, all the birds over a wide expanse of country will see the falcon "waiting on" at a very high pitch, but only the individual covey put up for her will be disturbed. Of course, it must be admitted that the ground is left *entirely* undisturbed for much longer periods when shot over than when hawked.

Peregrines flying over have the effect of making game birds lie close. Eagles have just the opposite effect. In Scotland it is well known how the appearance of an eagle over the skyline will clear a whole glen of grouse - to the great discomfiture of driving operations that may be in progress. The grouse will come back again soon, it is true, but many a day's shooting has been spoilt, or partly spoilt, by the presence of an eagle.

The peregrine takes its prey on the wing, and the game birds seem to have developed to a high degree the power of distinguishing between the ground-hunting eagle and buzzard, and the falcon. In her presence they exhibit the different reaction of lying close. Duck, curlew, gulls - all are prey for the peregrine; her powers of sight are very great and she may make a flight of miles to knock a bird more or less dead to the ground or, "trussing" it, carry it to some convenient place to eat at her leisure.

Where a peregrine inhabits a sea-cliff near colonies of puffins, flights are made along the cliff face and a puffin flying forth or coming home is sure to fall victim. These birds are often taken to a dub of water and thoroughly wetted before the peregrine plucks them. The reaction of lying close in the presence of the falcon is nothing like so highly developed in cliff-breeding birds as in game, though black guillemots or tysties when attacked over the sea will fall like stones to the water and disappear below the surface.

The falcon receives a good deal of inadvertent help in getting grouse flushed for her by the passage of a shepherd or his dogs over the ground, a stalker or a gillie with a pony, or even innocent people searching for white heather. A peregrine does not wait for weak or sickly birds to get up, but goes for the first seen on a covey rising. I have many times seen trained peregrines kill the leading bird of a covey of grouse or partridges, and if a trained bird will do this it seems reasonable to suppose a wild bird would do the same. Healthy birds are much the more likely to be first on the wing than the sickly ones.

The so-called balance of nature, which in truth is not so much a balance as a see-sawing, pendulum-like movement, is inevitably much upset in civilised countries, for certain predatory animals have to be kept in check in order to maintain flocks and herds and even the amenities of settled life. We "farm" our game birds and animals to some extent, and to ensure a more or less steady crop some of the predatory species have at least to be lessened. There has been a steady advance towards an enlightened policy of game preservation, and we may hope the future will see all keepers, lessees and proprietors conserving game with greater knowledge of the true role of some animals and birds which formerly shamed the vermin pole. Long may the peregrine falcon persist in a world of live and let live!

Peregrine falcon engraving, by G.E. Lodge.

51

Field Sketch Books

T he Trust is most privileged to have within its holdings a number of George Lodge's field sketch books, which were kindly donated.

These are extremely varied in their subject matter and date from the 1890s to 1940s. Among them are a few relating to hawking and depict many of the past falconer's hawks. George Lodge had the ability to capture the characters of each hawk individually with a pencil stroke, which demonstrates his sharp observation and immense talent as an artist falconer. The sketches are of hawking days on Bodmin Moor in Cornwall, Islay, Scotland and Salisbury Plain in Wiltshire.

G.E.L. Trust

'Diana', a peregrine falcon – 30th September 1936.

aug 4. 1939.

Merlin sketches – 4th August 1939.

Lindsey.
aug. 11. 1936.

'Lindsey', a peregrine falcon – 11th August 1936.

'Lindsey II', a peregrine falcon – 15th August 1936.

Helga

Aug. 12 1936

Aug.24.39.
Salisbury Plain.

Box cadge of hooded peregrines on Salisbury Plain – 24th August. 1939.

Photographs

The photographs share a special window of the past, especially George Lodge's relationship with the Mann family. They give us an insight into this time-honoured sport, that meant so much to them.

Thomas Mann had his own private hawking establishment, his home and hawk mews were at Hyde Hall, Sawbridgeworth, Hertfordshire. He employed a full-time professional falconer, Alfred Frost who showed excellent sport in the field; rook hawking on the borders of Essex and Cambridgeshire, and game hawking with peregrines in Norfolk. The hawking season in August also consisted of the training and flying of merlins. George Lodge was a regular visitor to Hyde Hall, and so much so, he became known by the Mann family as 'Uncle Dick', short for dicky bird!

G.E.L. Trust

George Lodge with peregrine, standing in the grounds of Hyde Hall, 1894.

Thomas Mann with his professional falconer Alfred Frost mounted on hawking pony.

T. J. Mann's hawking party in the 1880s or 1890s, but most probably the latter. Top left-hand corner stands Alfred Frost holding a goshawk (Shadow of Death?). George Lodge is seated second from bottom right, next to Thomas Mann.

George Lodge with gyr-falcon, 1936.

Time out from hawking with the Mann family at Hyde Hall, Sawbridgeworth.
Left to right on top row – George Lodge, Percy or Hugh Mann?, Thomas Mann, and
Leonard Jorgensen. Middle row – third from the left, wife of Thomas Mann, and fourth from
the left is his daughter Winifred.

T.J. Mann's cadge of falcons, 1888.

G.E. Lodge in his Camberley studio during 1951 with 2 mounted falcons, 'Celia' & 'Farthingale'.

'Celia' Intermewed falcon trained and entered to rooks by the Old Hawking Club. Later flown by T.J. Mann at rooks in Cambs 1890-91. Remounted by George Lodge 06/11/34.

'Farthingale' Intermewed falcon trained and entered to rooks by the Old Hawking Club. Later flown at rooks and Norfolk plover (caught 7 of latter) in Cambs 1889. Remounted by George Lodge 08/11/34.

61

Memorabilia

The Trust is most fortunate to have within its holdings a variety of donated memorabilia that belonged to George Lodge.

Among them are George Lodge's falconer's gauntlet and gravers that form part of the collection, these establish his own relationship with falconry. The gauntlet is well-used and may have had many a famous hawk perched upon it. The gravers probably date back to the 1880s and were possibly used for the illustrations throughout 'MODERN FALCONRY'. George Lodge had become an extremely expert wood engraver and one can find some very fine examples of his engraving in such books as J.G. Millais's 'Breath from the Veldt' 1899 and 'Game Birds and Shooting Sketches' 1892.

Thomas Mann's falconer's gauntlet was a great find during some recent research work. It links together with the photograph of Thomas Mann that appears on the 'Dedication' page where he can be seen wearing the very same gauntlet. This is the same style as seen in the famous 'Black Jess' painting.

G.E.L. Trust

George Lodge's gravers, well-used and re-ground marked with his initials GEL.

George Lodge's falconer's gauntlet.

Dutch Hood Silver Mustard Pot

This Dutch Hood Silver Mustard Pot is one of a limited edition of (4). These beautifully made replicas of falcon hoods were privately commissioned by George Lodge for his close hawking companions. Lodge oversaw their immense quality and detail. Even the spoons have been meticulously designed and made to resemble a pair of lure wings, which are attached to the lure line

Each silver hood is numbered at the base from (1) to (4). Number (4) was in the possession of George Lodge himself, until his death in 1954.

Dutch Hood

The Mollen family, were professional hawk-catchers and falconry furniture suppliers of Eindhoven, Holland – and made the Dutch Hood for European falconers.

Before and after the First World War a number of red passage peregrine falcons were obtained from Valkenswaard, Holland. These often made first class rook and game hawks for falconers. The Mollen family netted the peregrines on migration in the autumn. The Old Hawking Club and Hawking Establishments of the past, including T.J. Mann's, ordered fresh passage hawks every season.

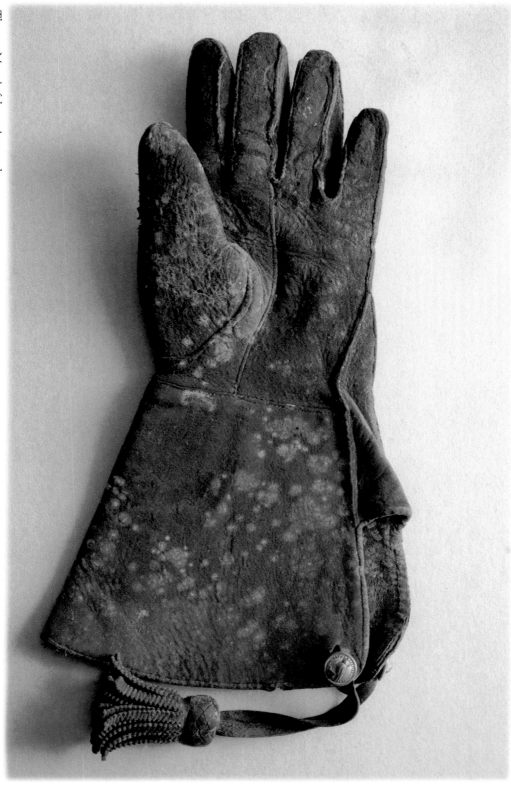

Thomas Mann's falconer's gauntlet.

'Black Jess', oil painting by G.E. Lodge.
Intermewed eyass falcon. Trained and flown by the late Kim Muir, 10th Royal Hussars.

GLOSSARY OF HAWKING TERMS

Bate : a hawk "bates" when struggling to fly from fist or block.

Bind : to clutch and hold the quarry in the air, instead of giving it a knock-out blow.

Blue hawk : a peregrine in adult "blue" plumage.

Cadge : a wooden frame on which falcons are carried hooded to the field.

Check : to "check" is to leave the quarry flown at for another.

Eyass : a young hawk taken from nest.

Falcon : female peregrine or gyr. Also applied to other long-winged falcons, such as Saker, Lanner, Shahîn, etc.

Foot : a hawk is a good or a bad "footer" according to her ability or otherwise to hit or to catch her quarry.

Hack : young hawks taken from nest are kept at "hack," which is complete liberty until the time that they must be put into training.

Haggard : a wild-caught hawk in adult plumage.

Intermewed : a hawk that has moulted in captivity.

Jack : the male merlin.

Jesses : the short leather thongs that are permanently fixed to the hawk's legs.

Lure : a leather pad garnished with a couple of wings, tossed into the air at the end of a line, used to bring down hawks to the falconer after unsuccessful flight; also used for training purposes.

Man : to man a hawk is to make it tame. A well-"manned" hawk will sit quietly on fist, unhooded, showing no fright or distress of strange lights and noises.

Merlin : the female merlin.

Musket : the male sparrowhawk.

Out of the hood : flying a peregrine, or other long-winged hawk direct from the fist at quarry.

Passage hawk : a hawk caught wild in its immature plumage.

Pitch : the height that a hawk attains in the air while "waiting on."

Put in : a quarry "puts in" to cover to escape pursuing hawk.

Plume : a hawk "plumes" her quarry when plucking it.

Quarry : the game flown at.

Rake away : a hawk leaving its quarry and flying away.

Red hawk : a peregrine in its immature plumage.

Sparrowhawk : female sparrowhawk.

Stoop : the downward plunge of a hawk on to its quarry.

Tiercel, or tercel : the male of peregrine or gyr, and kindred long-winged hawks.

Truss : same as to "bind."

Waiting-on : a hawk circling overhead waiting for quarry to be flushed.

Weather : hawks on their blocks in the open air are "weathering."

There are many more technical falconry terms; but the above will suffice for this book.

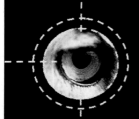

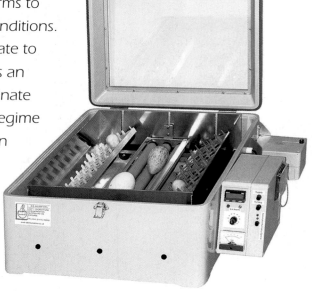